"He has an infectious personality, an abundance of ... r-nation and speed to burn. I really enjoy the zeal he exhibits for life. His story is one of sacrifice, inspiration, and perseverance." —*Jim Caldwell, NFL head coach of the Indianapolis Colts*

"Frank has made a tremendous impact on me and our players. Frank's love for Jesus transcends his wealth of knowledge about football, and that alone has helped our team to elevate our expectations and our performance. Frank's message and testimony will only inspire and uplift your spirit." —*Phil Massey, head football coach, Baylor School*

"Passion and perseverance are the traits that come to mind when I think of my friend Frank Murphy. When I talk to my young players about what it takes to make yourself a critical part of the team, I recall men like Frank, who sacrificed and worked with a winning attitude each day to make his team's success." —*Coach Rasheed Morris, NFL head coach of the Tampa Bay Buccaneers*

"It is truly remarkable to see the transformation in Frank's life. He has been a true friend and a great model for kids to look up to." —*Brian Kelly, NFL former All Pro Cornerback for the Tampa Bay Buccaneers*

"God has so much love for us all. Frank had a Damascus experience as he was growing up in life. God met him on that Damascus road and He changed his life that day and ever since he has been favored by God. Frank's love for God's people goes far and beyond what one can imagine. Frank's talent on the football field without a doubt ranks as the best I've seen during my thirty-five years of coaching at West Nassau." —*Coach Johnnie Green, West Nassau High School*

"It's still Murph Tyme!" —*Warren Sapp, former NFL All Pro Defensive Lineman for the Tampa Bay Buccaneers*

"I have followed Frank's playing career for several years. His talent and strong work ethic has led to a dynamic and lengthy football career. As talented as he is, he is an even greater asset to our community. During his time with the Buccaneers, Frank was always a leader when it came to giving back to the area. To this day, he is still active with various causes in the Tampa area. Having the talent to play football at a professional level is a special gift. What sets Frank apart is what he has done with that gift both on and off the field." —*Former AFL Champ Coach Tim Marcum, Tampa Bay Storm*

"Frank always seemed to have a permanent smile on his face…many players nicknamed him 'He-He', as if he was laughing internally. The reality of his smile is that he enjoys life, enjoys teammates, and enjoys the competition of football. As a special teams player, Frank was outstanding, an explosive returner and a dominant coverage player. He used a phrase I still use today, 'trim the fat,' which means bring that speed off the edge." —*Joe Marciano, NFL special teams coach for the Houston Texans*

"Frank has a tremendous testimony of God's grace in his life and does a wonderful job of communicating that message. His willingness to share with young athletes and to influence them toward the Christ he knows and loves has made a significant impact in our area and in others where Frank has lived." —*Jay Fowler, Fellowship of Christian Athletes, Chattanooga, TN*

"I enjoyed seeing Frank grow as a person and student as well as witnessing his mother's appreciation for the direction he had taken in life. Frank was a very talented football athlete, but I was and am most impressed by his growth as a genuine, caring, sincere, passionate, and faithful person. He has been and will continue to be successful." —*Bill Snyder, head coach of Kansas State University*

"I have known Frank Murphy for a number of years and during this time, I have witnessed him bring an unparalleled amount of energy and passion to teaching kids the game of football. His focus on sharing life lessons and motivating young athletes to do their best has made him a true asset to not only ProCamps, but the communities that we impact." —*Gregg Darbyshire, Chief Executive – ProCamps Worldwide*

"There is no doubt in my mind that God has His hand on Frank's life. God has given this young man a heart for righteousness and a steadfast desire for growth through God's Word. Frank's zeal to be what God has ordained him to be is a beautiful thing to watch. It is amazing to see how God has blessed Frank through the struggles and gifted him to serve and be a testimony of the goodness of God's grace and

mercy. I am confident that every reader will be inspired by this book and finish with a vision of what God can do in a young man's life."
—*Evangelist RV Brown, Exec. Director of Outreach To America's Youth, Inc., Author, Speaker*

"Congratulations Murph! It has been a privilege and an honor representing you as your agent. The relationship we have built over the years will remain with me forever. Your dedication to football and your drive to succeed should serve as an inspiration to all young kids today. As your agent, seeing you reach your goals and dreams is very rewarding. All of us at MRM Sports & Entertainment are proud of you! Best wishes, always."
—*Marty Magid, Agent, MRM Sports & Entertainment*

THE MAN
BEHIND
THE HELMET

...and the God of
second chances

FRANK D. MURPHY

Mobile, Alabama

Cover Photography/Interior Photography: ROC Studios International, Inc.

ISBN 978-1-58169-392-8
For Worldwide Distribution
Printed in the U.S.A.

Evergreen Press
P.O. Box 191540 • Mobile, AL 36619
800-367-8203
http://christian-publishing.net

Contents

Frank gives God the glory after a Tampa Bay Buccaneers touchdown

To my loving father, Franklin Dover Murphy Sr.
Rest in peace. He was the rock of my life
and my family life. Man, that guy worked hard!
Thanks, Dad.

To all the people who made mistakes
and thought it was over—it's not!
Step up, step out, and step forward, my friend—
It's YOUR time!

I saved the best for last:
To my Lord and Savior, Jesus Christ, God, the Holy
Spirit, has brought me through every trial and mistake
that I ever made in my life. That's a true and real Friend.
Now I understand unconditional and agape love at its
best—thank You, Jesus, for dying for me.

Frank D. Murphy, NFL Wide Receiver and Kick Return Specialist, Tampa Bay Buccaneers

Special Thanks

To my number-one source, God, my Lord and Savior, Jesus Christ. To Frankie D. Murphy III, Isaiah Murphy, Miracle Murphy, and Ameer Murphy. To my mother, Velma Murphy, my rock and prayer warrior for my life's success; you have always been my cheerleader and best friend ever—thanks, Mom! To my father, for his hard work and giving spirit—rest in peace, Red. To my sisters and brothers: Cherisa, Rolanda, Cheryl, Joseph, Joshua, and Reginald, and all of the Jones and Murphy family; thank you for your love and support and for believing in me. To the NFL teams: Chicago Bears, Tampa Bay Buccaneers, Miami Dolphins, and the Houston Texans— thank you for the opportunity of a lifetime.

Thanks to the UFL, Florida Tuskers, and CFL Toronto Argonauts for the opportunity to play among such fine people. To the West Nassau High School coaches and teachers who stood by my side. Thanks to Itawamba and Garden City Community College for the opportunity to succeed. Thanks to Kansas State University, and all the fans, teachers, and coaches who believed in me. To Tony Gaskins, thanks for your obedience to the Holy Spirit in helping me to complete this book; to the D1 training facility for the opportunity to train and impact athletes and health enthusiasts of all ages and genders, to Baylor School for the opportunity to impact young lives, to Pro Camps Worldwide for the opportunity to train and impact youth.

To the Brown family for your support and love; the Baker family for legal support and sound advice; to Mrs. Cheryl for her spiritual guidance at Garden City Community College, rest in peace; to Pastors Michael and Connie Smith of the Church Group Worldwide for teaching the Word in simplicity in the time of need. To my spiritual father and mother, Pastors Greg and Deborah Powe, for your spiritual guidance and leadership ability, and most importantly for revealing the truth to me in love—you are my friends forever. Also to Revealing Truth Ministries, my church family.

To my cousins Maurice Brailsford and Lisa McClendon-Brailsford, who gave me encouraging words in hard times; to Kirk Gradelle for financial wisdom and friendship; to Winston Jackson, for your brotherhood and friendship; to Michael Tally, for being the truth teller in my life; to my friend Terrence Flemings, a great covenant friend of mine. To Robert and Shantae Charles, for a great project walking the faith journey with me and for letting patience have its perfect work; I couldn't have asked for a better couple.

If I left anyone out, charge it to my head and not my heart. You all have impacted my life and made an indelible imprint on my heart. Without your influence, I would not have made it or become the man I am. Remember, believe it! Claim it! Work it out!

Preface

The Spirit of God has inspired Frank to share with the world parts of his life. Everyone needs a second chance. In golf they call it a mulligan. If you've ever wanted a do-over, then this inspiring story about forgiveness and second chances is the shot of grace you have been looking for. In these pages, you will learn a lot about life, decisions, and right relationships.

When Frank joined our church years ago, his life was in disarray. Over the years it became clear that the Word that God was speaking through me began to impact his life in a very great way. His commitment to consistently coming to church, and not only being one who *hears* the Word but *does* the Word, is what has enabled him to overcome every obstacle in his life. I truly believe this book will be a blessing to anyone who reads it.

As you take this journey with Frank and understand how he persevered, you'll find that he became much more than an athlete but a transformed man of God. May you find that same grace to change course.

Pastor Greg Powe
Revealing Truth Ministries
Tampa, FL

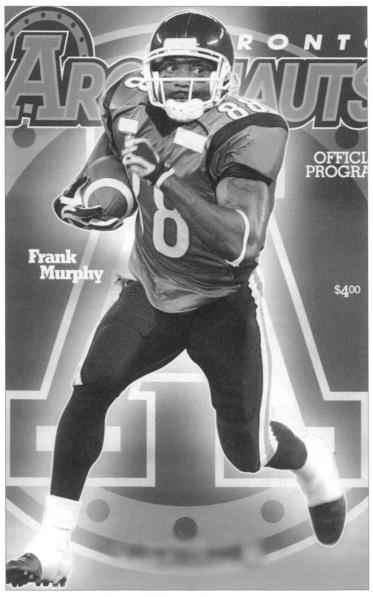

Frank D. Murphy, Toronto Argonauts Wide Receiver #88

Foreword

In September of 2000 I had my first meeting with Frank Murphy. At that time I was the Head Coach of the Tampa Bay Buccaneers, and Frank was a rookie player that our scouts recommended we sign to a contract. They told me he had a world of talent but was still somewhat raw as a football player. They also told me he had been in a little trouble in the past but had tremendous potential that hadn't been fully developed yet. I found out they were right on both counts!

As I got to spend time with Frank, I found out that he had come from a troubled past. He, like so many of our young men today, had fallen into the trap of chasing the wrong things with the wrong people. Some of the decisions he had made left some grave consequences, but Frank told me he was determined to move forward and change the way he approached life. All he needed, he told me, was another chance.

I believed in him, but those changes would be difficult and they wouldn't happen overnight. I gave him a chance to be on our team in Tampa, but it was God who really gave Frank a "second chance" at life. Over the next few years he got to see that you don't measure life by material things and that you only fool yourself when you chase the wrong things in life. While playing professional football once seemed to be the ultimate dream for him, he actually discovered that it doesn't profit a man anything to gain the whole world and forfeit his soul.

As I said, that growth didn't come instantly and Frank had to learn some hard lessons before he finally changed his lifestyle and committed his life totally to God. But there was always that good side to him—the side that made you root for him and really wish for him to succeed. With this book Frank is hoping to do the one thing he has always wanted to do and that's to help others. He wants to show people how God made a change in his life and helped him realize what it means to have the right priorities.

It's my hope that young people will read this book and be encouraged—not to follow the unstable path of chasing after the things much of our society says are important, but encouraged to chase the right dreams and follow the Lord's guidance. And encouraged to follow Frank Murphy's example of never giving up. I hope they will see, as Frank did, that it is only through Christ that they can reach their potential!

—*Tony Dungy, Former Superbowl NFL coach and player*

Frank D. Murphy, Kansas State University Running Back #3

Casual Frank—"Murph Tyme"

1

FAKE ID

"Some of y'all will be dead, on drugs, selling drugs, or in jail."
—Frank's Little League football coach,
Jacksonville, FL

Only the Strong Survive

The door slammed behind me as I entered the sixth floor of the Duval County Jail escorted by guards, hands chained in front of me, and leg shackles making music with every step. All I could hear were voices screaming at me along the way.

"What are you doin' here, Frank? I thought you played ball. You don't belong here, Superstar. What's wrong with you?"

The rank smell of old socks and mildew suffocated me and hung in the air. The paint-chipped walls felt as if they were closing in on me. The desperate and hopeless gazes seemed to burn through to my core. Everyone wanted to know what I, Mr. Frank D. Murphy Jr., the Superstar Athlete, was truly made of and what had gone wrong in my life to land me in jail.

As I entered the mess hall and got my tray of food, I quietly went to sit down trying to keep to myself. All that was going through my mind was my need to survive. Forehead beading with sweat, palms moist, heart racing, and mind boggled, I was living a nightmare. I had not foreseen these events. From that point on, things would be different for me.

For the next three days, I couldn't eat a bite of food. Constantly on the lookout for predators, I couldn't focus on anything else. My eyes were wide open and attentive to the movements of everything around me. I had no idea what I had gotten myself into and the depravity I would witness. I saw drugs being distributed, shanks being made, guys striking fires and smoking through batteries, devices being made that would confuse anyone on the outside. Here, in the place created for delinquents, lay undiscovered talent going down the drain, inventions that would never be patented for good but simply made to help a man survive in the slammer. I was a witness to the wasted potential of those who had been given up on— including me.

At night when I would lie down to try to sleep, all I could think about was how I had ended up here. As I listened I could hear guys crying, and I shed some tears of my own. This was the only time I felt safe because I was locked up by myself, and no one and nothing could get to me through those bars except the thoughts that bombarded my restless mind.

Outside my cell there was no solace, only chaos and confusion. Imagine having to shower in front of other guys whom you've never met before in your life. On top of that, there were adult men who had to watch us shower. The lack of privacy went beyond the shower. I even had to use the restroom in the open. No matter what activity, there was no privacy. This wasn't the life I was used to.

I didn't want to eat, but finally the hunger overtook me, and my body demanded that I eat the slop they referred to as food. You really didn't know what it was you were eating on some days, but I did know I had to eat to live. On top of having to settle for "mystery meat," I had to eat it at speeds unheard of. Running out of time and running out of calm, I just had to survive.

As time went on, people seemed to think there was something special about me. Brown-skinned, clean-cut, and muscularly built, I was not the largest person on the block, but I had gained respect. On one hand, I had become a vicious, quick-tempered enforcer; on the other hand, I was caring, understanding, and protective. I was seen as the leader of my cell block. I grabbed respect on the first day I walked into the Duval County Jail, and I had no intention of losing it.

I quickly became friends with the guards and charmed them with my million-dollar smile. I couldn't put it on for long, just long enough to win some favor and keep my head above water. I started receiving extra food from the guards and distributing it among the weaker guys. I took weaklings, or "ducks" as the inmates called them, under my wing and made sure they ate their meals every day. In order to keep getting extra food and privileges from the guards, I had to keep my cell block under control. Under my reign, there weren't any riots or out-of-control fights, unless I saw fit. Everybody ate and everybody knew who was in charge.

Although my leadership showed up in a place many wouldn't believe leaders existed, it was a foreshadowing that I can only attribute to what God had in store for me. I was a leader and I didn't even realize it.

Some this call is thrust upon them, some are born into it, and some are born with it. I discovered I was born with this ability to lead, and it became instrumental to my life at this time.

As I served my year in jail, I adapted to my environment. It was survival of the fittest, so I made sure I was fit. I sharpened my mind by reading encouraging letters and books. I toned my body by doing pushups, sit-ups, and curls with my mattress. I never knew when another test would come, but I did know I had to be ready.

Although my leadership showed up in a place many wouldn't believe leaders existed, it was a foreshadowing that I can only attribute to what God had in store for me. I was a leader and I didn't even realize it.

In order to keep my mind occupied, I would rap. I would gather my crew, and we would play cards and tell jokes. I did what I had to do to adapt to the environment, just like an animal in the wild. I would make it home, and I never lost hope of seeing the light of day again. If convicted, I would face five to ten years in prison. For me, that simply wasn't an option.

There were times when I would be allowed to go back to what I knew best: sports. We were given recreation time in which we would play basketball on an inside court because we were on the sixth floor of the jail. There wasn't much sunlight, only little peepholes that allowed some natural light to shine through. On the court there was a musky aroma that lingered and it became second nature to smell after a while. That place became another safe haven for me. On occasion we could make it through a game or two without fights breaking out, and during those times, I couldn't have been more content. As one of the few inmates who could dunk the almost eleven-foot goals, I literally soared above the rest. It made me stand out in the crowd.

There was a basketball coach from a neighboring high school who would come and watch me play, and he was stumped by my athletic ability—a young kid barely six feet tall, dunking an almost eleven-foot goal. That coach told me that when I got out of Duval

County Jail, he wanted me to come and start for his high school basketball team. Although it sounded good, I had other things on my mind.

Beyond the court, there was family. Coming from two loving and caring parents, I realized I had something many of my fellow inmates didn't have. If they played Little League sports, some had that Pop Warner Coach who served in the place of an absentee father. I didn't realize how important that love and support was, though, until one day when my mom came to visit. I had always been an optimist; no matter how dark it was, I saw the light at the end of the tunnel. That was how I saw my upcoming trial. The thought that one day I would be free again gave me hope.

The sad part is that things don't always come as easy as we would wish. Over and over again I would go to court with high hopes, and I would return broken in spirit after my trial was postponed again, and again, and yet again. Many believe it is a trick of the system to break us as young men to teach us a lesson, especially if the court knows the prosecution doesn't have enough evidence to punish us. At the time I wasn't thinking that way. All I wanted was to see the light of day again.

One day after a court hearing, I returned to my cell block disappointed that there still wasn't a decision made on my case. With that pent-up anger, I let my mother have it during our visitation session. I was so enraged and upset because she didn't seem to understand my pain and frustration, not realizing that her hands were tied and totally disregarding that it was my own bad decisions that had led me to my current state. I got up and began to storm off after brutally yelling at my loving, caring, and praying mother.

The guard who was standing nearby monitoring the visit yelled at me: "Hey, boy, SIT BACK DOWN! That's your MOTHER! I know it's hard in here, but she is here for YOU! You can't be mad at her! Don't ever disrespect her when she is here supporting YOU!"

> "Hey, boy, SIT BACK DOWN! That's your MOTHER! I know it's hard in here, but she is here for YOU! You can't be mad at her! Don't ever disrespect her when she is here supporting YOU!"

I turned around and went back to sit down. From that day forward, I never disrespected my mother again. From that moment on, I began to count my blessings and realize that she didn't have to be there for me. So many other mothers had abandoned their sons in my position. I realized that she didn't have to keep putting money in my commissary account so that I could have extra food and snacks to eat. I saw that not everyone had a mother and for those who did, not many had one like mine.

Rewind about fifteen or sixteen years: I was born to Velma and Franklin D. Murphy Sr. on the appointed day of February 11 in Jacksonville, Florida. "Bang 'Em," or Duval County, is known to many as the Murder Capital of Florida. This is a place where parents can do everything in their power to raise their children right and still lose them to the street life. I was one of five children born to a middle-class family, so the focus was divided and the pressures were even greater than in a smaller family. For fourteen years, Franklin Sr. and Velma were successful at raising their son, but there came a day that would change me forever.

I was about twelve years old, quiet and shy, not street-savvy, and I was far from a troublemaker. I was just a young man living life the best way I knew how. But on one humid, sun-scorched day in Florida, the long walk home would turn out to be a walk I wouldn't forget. As I was walking home, a group of thugs ran up behind me. One of them grabbed my legs in a fast sweep and flipped me over onto my back. Then he pounced down on top of me as if he were about to beat me up!

What made him stop? Only God and that boy

knew. But he didn't hit me. Instead he got up, and I got up and ran for home while the guy and his friends had a kick out of scaring me. I believe I was targeted by these bullies because I was seen as weak, different, an outcast, and a good guy. In a sense, it was that boy's inner battle with frustration and lack of self-worth that rubbed off on me. From that day forward I would never be the same. I went home and looked in the mirror. With tears in my eyes, I promised myself that I would not let anyone hurt me again. I began studying the streets. I got into street and hood music, trying to understand their thoughts, their struggles, and their pain.

I took on their lifestyle—the complete opposite of my well-grounded upbringing. I put on a hard exterior. It was my new ID, only it was fake—I was a total fraud, but I wanted to be the real thing. This was my fake ID.

> It was my new ID, only it was false—I was a total fraud, but I wanted to be the real thing. This was my fake ID.

I became someone completely different. Not only did my parents and siblings not recognize me, but I didn't even recognize myself.

This lifestyle sent me spiraling out of control. I began to get into guns and drugs. I wanted to understand how guns worked, how the drug game worked, and how the streets worked in general. Thugs became my best friends. The guys with no parents or drug-addicted parents became my friends. I no longer identified with the "good life." All I wanted to understand was the "thug life." I was indoctrinated by my new friends, only I wasn't ready yet for Hard Knocks University.

I went on from middle school to high school and continued living the thug lifestyle. I began hanging out and selling drugs. I took on the thug mentality. My environment began to decline, and I was brought down too. The peace and happiness I experienced at home weren't the same gifts that the streets had to give. I went into survival mode. I felt that in order to survive in the streets, love and happiness weren't the goals I needed. I adapted to my surroundings and found a way to get ahead out there.

Guns, drugs, and violence were a way of life for the youth in my neighborhood, and I felt that in order to make it out alive I had to get in where I'd fit in. My elders always said, "You'll be like what you hang around." One thing led to another, and I found that saying to be true firsthand. Although I was changing into an unrecognizable person and flaunting my fake ID, there were still some things about me that my new lifestyle couldn't change—a giving and caring heart, for one.

My less-fortunate friends would come over to my home to hang out. I would conveniently have them stay over until dinnertime and pretend it was an accident, but in all honesty I did it so they could have something to eat.

Beyond the food, I would pretend I didn't want certain clothes in my closet or pretend they were too small for me, and then pass them on to my less-fortunate friends. I wanted to keep these character traits dormant in me, yet in the midst of the bad, the good was still trying to wrestle its way to the surface.

There was a war going on inside of me, the battle of good versus evil. This was spiritual warfare, but no one knew it at the time except my praying mother. The devil saw those godly traits in me and knew that if they were allowed to flourish, I would become a leader for God unlike this world had ever seen before. So he set out to stomp out that seed that was planted in my heart from a young age. My mother said to me that from the day I was born she knew I would be great one day. She had visions of me traveling the world and ministering the Gospel, but she knew in order for it to come to pass she would have to remain in constant prayer for me.

There was a time when my mother spanked me for the last time, and I didn't budge or cry. From that moment on she knew that she had to enter into intercessory prayer for me because the devil was trying to hinder the gifts that God had given me.

As a very little boy I could be found in the backyard from time to time pretending to be preaching the Gospel of Jesus Christ. Then I would play it off as if nothing were happening if anyone came around the corner. The devil saw these signs and set out to ruin me before I ever got started. I was on a road leading to nowhere at breakneck speed into a head-on collision with tragedy. No one could stop me, and nothing could keep me from the impact but the grace of God.

> I was on a road leading to nowhere at breakneck speed into a head-on collision with tragedy. No one could stop me, and nothing could keep me from the impact but the grace of God.

Fast-forward to my time in the Duval County Jail. After being straightened out by the guard at the jail, I began to see my support system a little differently. I put that love in a jar and bottled it up for times of need, but I knew I still had to survive in that jail where motherly love didn't exist. There was no one holding my hand, fretting over me, and bandaging my bruises with care. It was hard. I continued to run my cell block and maintain the respect of the other inmates. I didn't back down for anybody, and I made sure I stood up for the weak. I would befriend the guys whom no one else would talk to. Of course I had to put on a certain demeanor to do it, but I was able to show love in a tough way.

I continued to run my cell block and maintain the respect of the other inmates. I didn't back down for anybody, and I made sure I stood up for the weak.

During my jail time, some guys came in who were accused of killing a girl because she was the pregnant girlfriend of one of the guys. She was set up and beaten with a brick to kill the baby, but they allegedly killed her too. The word was out that the guys were coming, and it wasn't going to be pretty for them when they got in. I didn't condone what they had done, but I understood the principle of forgiveness. It was that trait in me that would allow me to overlook the wrong that these young men were accused of doing and befriend them in order to help them keep their sanity.

I would sneak and talk to guys like them and tell them that everything would be okay and that God would forgive them. I would look out for them and always give them a word of encouragement. I felt as if I had been put in a position of power to serve and protect, as ironic as it sounds. I was just doing what came naturally to me.

It was impossible for me to have so much love instilled in me and not carry some of that love inside the prison. It was there, and it showed up no matter how much I tried to hide it. I stayed out of trouble for the most part and did everything I was supposed to do because I knew my trial day was coming soon.

Imagine serving almost a year for a crime you swore you didn't commit. Then the judgment day came and your whole life flashed before your eyes. I entered the courtroom not knowing what my fate would be. All I had was hope that I would get another chance at life. As I entered, I broke out into a sweat and my hands began to shake. I looked over and saw my mother's prayerful posture, and it gave me a little extra strength.

As I stood to hear the verdict read, the words "not guilty" rang out, and joy poured over me, chills running up and down my body. The sweetest words I had heard in a long time came from a complete stranger who held the key to my future.

I knew God had granted me a chance to get it right. I was released later that day, and as I walked out, the sun seemed to hit me. I almost fell to the ground, released from the weight of incarceration and overwhelmed with joy to see the light of day as a free man! No one but God knew what was in store for me, but I would soon find out.

2

SECOND
CHANCES

"Frank, there is
something special
about you, I know it."
—Ms. Cheryl, Garden City, KS

Senior Sensation

With a second chance at life, I wasted no time going back to what I knew—sports! I played basketball and football for West Nassau High School. Throughout high school I won numerous awards as the senior running back and return specialist, earning All-American, All State, and Player of the Year. Even though I had been released from jail, I still maintained a jail mindset. I had trouble looking at people as just individuals. I perceived everyone I came into contact with as a potential predator. I was constantly on guard and very uptight. This mind-set caused me to get into some fights after I got out because I wasn't able to discern between a true threat to my safety and a guy just trying to act tough. Nevertheless, I hung tight, realizing that a certain grace was over my life. As I look back, I recognize it was my mother's prayers that kept me safe.

> On the football field I felt like I was in heaven. The field was where I did everything right. The game I loved would change and save my life and prepare me for my future.

I was the star basketball player, football player, and track star for my high school. On the football field I felt like I was in heaven. The field was where I did everything right. There were no criminals, drugs, or any threats to my safety; it was only football. The game I loved would change and save my life and prepare me for my future.

I starred for my team and gained attention from all over. People asked, "Where did *he* come from?" I was the Senior Sensation! What looked to me like a new lease on life and a fresh start was innocently deceptive. There would be another obstacle that I would have to face—my academic life. I quickly realized how important it was to take school seriously. I had all the talent in the world, but I lacked the grades to get me into my university of choice. This was a very difficult lesson that I had to learn as a young man. As I mentor and coach, I try to drill home the concept of being a "student athlete" with the emphasis on student.

So many times young athletes shortchange their education, not realizing those skills will benefit them later as they manage their money, their careers, and the branding of their personalities as household names. I didn't have the grades to get into a big college, and I was on probation from other charges from another county. My past decisions were now narrowing my present choices. I went on to junior college. Though the colleges were seen as small, there were some big lessons to be learned from this experience.

Guilty by Association

Itawamba Community College was the name, and a second chance was the game. As I entered the city gates of Fulton, Mississippi, I thought, *This is where I will leave my troubles behind,* but I was in for a surprise. As is human nature, when we leave home we search for a home away from home, a place of familiarity. We tend to stick to what we know and just go with the flow. This is exactly what I decided to do.

Not knowing what to expect, but knowing I had to survive, I gravitated to guys who looked and sounded just like I did. It was a mind-set I needed to erase that influenced my attraction to those character traits. I hooked up with some friends and got sucked back in to the trap of the enemy. I began hanging out and having fun smoking and drinking and selling drugs to make a little extra money on the side. Many men can't understand what causes them to make those types of choices, but I attribute it to the fake ID. That is what was holding me down. With the desire to fit in by standing out, I led by example but followed a blind lead. The force that was driving me to return to my old ways was not understood at the time.

Trapped in the mind-set of the hood, it followed me like a shadow. Wherever I would go and whatever I would do, the street mentality lurked close by. "Survival of the fittest" and "getting in where you fit in" was what fueled me. I was still hotheaded and overly defensive as I kept running with my friends. There was one point during this time of my life when I went to a club and got into a fight. The losers in the fight weren't happy about it and began to shoot at us. It was another close call when God had His angels protecting me and I was not shot. However, it seemed like I just couldn't break the criminal mind-set.

Street Code

Where I'm from, there was a code, an unspoken understanding in the streets that many still abide by, and not snitching was a part of the code. I would be tested in this department sooner than I thought. It's sad to see one person suffer because of the guilt of another, but it's a price we pay when living by the "street code." Some of my friends got caught stealing, and I was pointed out as a witness and a suspect. Because I claimed innocence yet wouldn't reveal the guilty parties, I paid the same price as them. Part of gaining respect in the hood is through paying the price, taking the jail time, or doing other things that destroy your life's purpose to gain street cred.

Everyone who was associated with this theft, whether willingly or involuntary, was expelled from Itawamba Community College. This was a short-lived college experience, as it was only for six months. Even through such disappointing circumstances, there was an underlying trait that showed up clearly in this incident, and that was my faithfulness. Although this faithfulness was supplied to undeserving "friends," the fact still remains that it was evident.

> I denied myself and gambled with my future. Still the question remained: when would my virtue and good intentions be utilized for the right reasons?

I came to learn that although the "street code" exists, not many who are birthed into the game actually live the code. Many of the "street patrons," as I like to call them, will bail out at the first sign of trouble. Many of the original gangsters will leave their partners high and dry to save their own tails. By virtue of who I was, I brought with me a standard into a world where there is no virtue. This faithfulness went unnoticed and appreciated because in street life, faithfulness was out of place; it didn't belong in a world of players, schemes, setups, and cheats. This was a foreshadowing of my purpose, however. This was a sign of what I was meant to be: a person who could suffer the wrong for others and do it willingly. It's funny how that happens, but I was a prime example of it. Many seated in the witness chair would have given in to the pressure and the love of self. Instead, I denied myself and gambled with my future. Still the question remained: when would my virtue and good intentions be utilized for the right reasons?

Although I chose to give it all up and return home for some guys who probably wouldn't have done the same for me, my mother didn't feel the same way. She begged the coach not to send her baby home but rather assist him in transitioning to another college. The grace on her life flowed down to her son and the coach did just that. It wasn't long before the coach found another home for me and placed me on a bus out of nowhere going to nowhere. I got on the bus, feeling lonely and lost. The two days from Fulton, Mississippi, to Garden City, Kansas, seemed like the longest ride of my life! One would hope this ride would be a ride into change, but only God knew at that point.

Ready for the Call

Oftentimes when we are set in our ways, it takes a

huge jolt to shake us out of it. Something drastic, something life-changing, something nearly unbearable has to happen, but that jolt hadn't struck me yet. As I got off the bus in Garden City, Kansas, all I could smell was cows—hardly the smell of success! It was not the smell I was hoping for, but my mind began to prepare for what I thought was in store.

To my surprise I was able to run into guys who were just like me: guys who came from the same type of streets, lived the same type of life, and were headed the same place. The catch was that they didn't know where they were headed. Just like before, I reverted back to what I knew best. I had to make a name for myself: this was embedded in my "jail mentality." I had to run my cell, except in the real world I wasn't confined by four walls with tiny peepholes. This mentality could only get worse. It was only about three months before I found myself back on the drug scene making sales, trying to find myself by losing myself in making money. It wasn't what I had planned, but because I had failed to plan, it was where I found myself. With my chest poked out yet on guard, I was put to the test on a random night in a very unusual way.

That night I was falsely accused of being involved in a shootout. The reality of my circumstances hit me and I broke down. I was in the shower, the perfect place to cry because no one could tell the difference between the water and my tears. Beaten with guilt and shame, I cried out to God and asked Him to deliver me. I told God that if He would get me out of this bind, I would serve Him and do the right thing. It was almost as if that was all God was waiting for—for me to repent, to turn back to Him. I was released because they had no

> I cried out to God and asked Him to deliver me. I told God that if He would get me out of this bind, I would serve Him and do the right thing. It was almost as if that was all God was waiting for— for me to repent.

grounds to hold me at that time, but a trial was to come. When I was released, I had no one to call so I walked all the way home.

I was so happy to have another shot at life that I walked without even thinking about the distance, which was quite long. This time was different; this walk brought about a change. This time with God was cherished, and His Spirit ministered to me all the way home. A change had to come.

When I arrived back at the college, I had a meeting with the president of the college. God gave me favor with that man for some reason, and he didn't kick me out of the school, although my football coaches wanted me gone. The president said, "You are innocent until proven guilty, so you deserve the opportunity to continue pursuing your education." I took to heart the opportunity to remain in school, and I separated myself from that crowd and cut off those so-called friends who had helped me get into trouble.

I had a wilderness experience where I would be changed for a season. While on suspension, the college told me that I would have to pass twenty-four credits. This was a huge task at hand based on my academic past, but with the grace of God I was able to focus on business and complete this task. In that year of suspension, I passed those twenty-five credits and maintained a 3.2 GPA.

I was the same young man who didn't have the grades in high school to get into a Division 1 school. Yes, I was that same young man who had been discounted because of my grades, but I proved to myself and to others that I could do it.

At the end of that year I had to attend trial. Although I hadn't been on the team that year, my teammates still looked up to me and supported me. I went to trial and that same feeling came over me from my trial during high school. My teammates were tense about the whole trial, and they got on me about the seriousness of the charges, but I explained that I was at peace. I entered the courtroom with confidence rather than fear. I felt that confidence from above. I had made sacrifices, and I had changed my lifestyle. I was focused and developing into a new man, God had forgiven me for my past sins, and I had forgiven myself as well. Those around me who didn't understand my confidence were mind-boggled at the calm and upbeat attitude I displayed at a time when any other man would have been shaking with fear. I was nervous, but only God knew that. I had enough confidence in God that no one else could see my anxiety.

Those around me who didn't understand my confidence were mind-boggled at the calm and upbeat attitude I displayed at a time when any other man would have been shaking with fear.

The judge looked me in the eye and read the verdict: "Not guilty." Phew! I had made it out again. I had faced three to five years if I had been found guilty. A thunderous applause went up in the courtroom from my teammates and supporters who jumped for joy after the verdict, and I went home a free man.

My relief wouldn't last for long because the next step was to meet with my coaches. All of this personal drama had been a little too much for them. They called me into the office.

"Frank, we are going to have to let you go."

"No, Coach. You can't do that. That's not fair to me. I've come all this way, passed all of my classes, and won my trial, and now you say you're sending me home? I can't live with that."

I asked the coach to give me another shot. I told him that if I didn't make the team, then I would go home willingly. So by the grace of God, the coaches agreed to give me a shot to see if I was serious this time. I had no intentions of not making the team; I knew what I was capable of.

I went home that summer and got a job to put a little money in my pocket. I would get up in the morning, eat a champion's breakfast, go to work all day, and then get right back to my workout regimen. I would leave work rushing to the track. I would get to the track and run for a couple of hours. All the while I could hear the voice of my coaches in my head: "We're going to have to let you go." That fueled me and gave me the push I needed to train like there was no tomorrow. But here was the unexpected catch: there wasn't a position on the team for me. I had been a running back all of my life, but there was an all-American running back ahead of me who had just rushed for over 2,000 yards the season before. This added to the pressure, but it wasn't enough pressure to make me give up. I was learning a life lesson: keep working hard, believing in God and yourself. Each day I would keep my training consistent with running and weights. I was becoming a Murphy Machine. My body began to swell and rip. I was getting ready for the call.

As the summer progressed, I was growing increasingly devoted and motivated. As I was winding down from a long, hard workout one day, I got a phone call. On the other end of the phone was a deep, stern voice that said, "Frank, I got some good news for you. The running back who was in front of you won't be returning next year due to some off-the-field issues."

My mouth dropped open. My heart racing with excitement, I responded with expectancy, "Okay, Coach, I'm ready!"

Support Systems

I got off the phone overwhelmed with joy. All the work I had done hadn't been in vain. This was a lesson that has continued to echo within me. I learned to always be ready for the call! I could have easily lost hope and

> I learned to always be ready for the call! I could have easily lost hope and doubted my return or my chance to play, but I didn't. I kept the faith and I worked as if I were the expected starter. I believed and I achieved my goal.

doubted my return or my chance to play, but I didn't. I kept the faith and worked as if I were the expected starter. I believed and I achieved my goal. It was as if God heard my prayers and saw my dedication. It seemed that those who were in the fore-front and were taking life for granted had run their course, just as I had done in the past.

I was staying out of trouble and keeping the promise I had made to God that lonely day in jail. The summer came to an end, and I was ready to return. No one knew what to expect but me.

At this small college in the middle of nowhere, I had to be my biggest supporter. I had to believe in myself when no one else would or could because I had not proven myself in this current arena. I learned to root for my own success. So I kept the faith and went out with the mind-set to prove everyone else wrong. The coaches didn't know what they were going to get that year. They didn't know if I would make it through the season without getting into trouble or suffering an injury. They didn't know if I would even cut it after being out for so long, but I knew, and that was motivation enough.

God had placed someone special in my life back in Garden City, Kansas. Her name was Ms. Cheryl (God rest her soul), and I loved her like a second mom. She was a custodian at my school, and we had passed each other on several occasions before we struck up a conversation. She said to me, "Frank, there is something special about you, I know it." It wasn't long before she became my backbone while I was in Garden City. She helped me keep my promise to God by getting me to church and by continually praying for me. She was a mom away from Mom and a rock that I could lean on. Ms. Cheryl would have me over to hang out with her own son as she took me under her wing. She was a heaven-sent angel.

With Ms. Cheryl by my side and my mind set on God, I was ready for my first season. I hit the ground running. I silenced the critics by staying out of trouble off the field and through an excellent performance on the field. I led my team in rushing as well as to the national championship game. Although we did not win the championship, I was named the MVP of the game. On top of that, I was named to the first team Junior College All-American. I was also voted the number one college recruit in the nation that year and was awarded the Junior College Heisman Trophy. This was an accomplishment that surpassed the imaginations of those around me.

When many expected me to screw up, somehow God said something different. By society's standard, these accomplishments should have put me on top of the world, but I remained grounded. I was humbled by my past experiences and all the long days and lonely nights in jail cells. I was humbled by the embarrassment and shame of my past. I had been through so much that this accomplishment wasn't bigger than hearing "not guilty" when I was facing five to ten years in prison. That was life; football was still just a game.

My true accomplishments were disciplining myself and surrounding myself with a good support system. After that season my name was in the mouths of many D1 Scouts. I began looking at my options and traveling around the country. I turned down several D1 universities in order to choose Kansas State University. I was offered to go to the CFL out of junior college. I was voted Pre Season Big 12 Newcomer of the Year.

3

IS LOVE PAIN

On one particularly intense play,
I took a wrong step and popped
a bone in my foot. "Why me?"
was all that I could say.

Loyal to the End

I am the type of man who follows his heart, and that is what I did when I made my decision to attend Kansas State University. There was something about Coach Bill Snyder that appealed to me and sealed the deal. But as soon as I got to school, there was a different kind of trouble waiting on me. It seemed that no matter what I did or where I went, I would face some type of trial to test my mettle.

It was revealed that I had booster friends who had been helping me out financially through school. Being that I wasn't familiar with the NCAA rules and regulations, I wasn't aware that accepting money from "friends" was illegal. I didn't see the boosters as boosters; I knew them as friends. I saw them as a "few good men" who were there for me when I needed them the most. I was called in by my coach and asked to roll over on the boosters who had helped me out.

I refused. My coach was baffled by the fact that I wouldn't tell him who these guys were, but it was just the code I lived by. I wasn't used to rolling over on anyone, and I wasn't about to start now. This wasn't about the streets; this wasn't about a G-code; this was just pure loyalty. I believed that you look out for those who have looked out for you. I was extremely frustrated because I couldn't understand why I was in trouble. I didn't see what was wrong with people helping me out when I was in need; as a neophyte, I just couldn't understand it.

The bigger picture was more complicated than I had thought; these boosters were there for me while I was at Garden City Community College and would look out for me financially whenever I needed the

> Had I been bought? Were the gifts and the money a snare, a hook, a lure to influence? Some would say yes, but ... my decision boiled down to the coach and his character.

funds. Years later, I decided to go to Kansas State University: these same guys turned out to be boosters of Kansas State. My life sounded as if it had been ripped straight from a movie script. I didn't realize it at the time, but the question was legitimate: Had I been bought? Were the gifts and the money a snare, a hook, a lure to influence? Some would say yes, but whether they contributed to my desire to attend Kansas State or not, for me, my decision boiled down to Coach Bill Snyder and his character and integrity.

So it came down to decision time. After speaking with the boosters, I was told to tell the coach who they were. I went back to my coach to tell him only because the boosters had given me permission because they didn't want to see me suffer. They admitted that they knew better and that they knew I was unaware of the regulations. I didn't feel like I had been bamboozled or tricked into anything because I actually needed the help I had been given.

I released the names and the decision on my punishment was decided. The school suspended me for two games and the NCAA tacked on two more games for a total of four games. This was a major blow for my first season at my new school, but it was better than having to be sent home. After the fourth week, I was getting ready to start my season when our quarterback made a prediction that I was going to take it all the way to the end zone on my first carry. Because of that prediction, my coach decided to sit me out the fifth game. He didn't want me under that much pressure to live up to the prediction.

Blow after blow, one after the other, kept coming, but I just kept rolling with the punches. My first year at Kansas State, my grandmother passed away. I had never seen my mom down like she was at that time. Those were trying times for me and my family, but with God's help we made it through. Finally I was able to get on the field for my junior season and I held my own. I ran hard and made a mark on my team, leaving an impression on my teammates and my opponents. I finished strong that season.

Love Is Pain

My junior season had ended and I was already preparing to go into Spring Training. Once again, I was about to face another test. In that Spring Training, I was going harder than ever. This was the time to prove myself to make sure my spot was secured for my senior season. On one particularly intense play, I took a wrong step and popped a bone in my foot. "Why me?" was all that I could say after this injury. Once again, I was being tested by some unknown force. Was it bad luck? Was I reaping what I had sown? Was it just pure coincidence? Or was this a setback for a setup? Was it an opportunity for a great comeback?

The doctor told me that I probably wouldn't be able to play until the fourth game of my senior season. With that in mind, I stayed in prayer that summer and was very careful with my sore foot. I had other plans, so I made sure I was on top of my rehab all the way through. I was able to make an earlier comeback and allowed to dress the first game of my senior season, even though I was not expected to play. A turn for the worse came for our team when the starting running back for that game fumbled the ball. My name was called.

I went into that game and rushed for over 140 yards making two touchdowns. Sometimes a turn for the worse can be your turn for the best.

I had gotten my steam back, and I was on a roll. I rolled through defenses week after week for the first three weeks, and then came the game against Texas. This was the fourth game of my senior season, and I was close in the standings to running back Heisman Trophy–winner Ron Dayne for the first three games. I was in the top five in rushing that year. This game against Texas would be one to remember for me because I was to be tested once again.

I was hyped and ready to play and got off to a good start. I was hoping that this game would help me close the gap on winning the Heisman, but I was in for a surprise. On an intense play, I was brought to a halt when I popped my ankle. All I could think was, *Wow, not again!* Yes, I was injured one more time. This was pretty incredible considering that after going all of my life without any injuries, my senior season seemed to be plagued by them. The game I loved brought me so much pain!

I was out for weeks with my injured ankle, but I decided not to lose faith and not to give up. I kept going, and I believed. I went into rehabilitation with the mind-set of working harder than ever to fully recover. I had to get back in time to play one more game. Because of my dedication and the grace of God, I was able to do just that. I made it back just in time for the *last* game of the senior season. Wow! What a way to finish my regular season.

Even though I was in pain, I still scored two touchdowns and got a standing ovation from the home crowd. After injury thought it had me down and out, I was able to bounce back and leave a lasting impression on the National League scouts.

I not only made it back to play that last game, but I was selected for an All-Star Game called the Gridiron Classic. I would have to trade reps with another running back in this game, but I was up for the challenge. I just had to do what I knew how to do, and that was run the ball.

For some reason I had a grace on my life and once again, the running back who was with me made a costly mistake—he fumbled the ball. For any player on the offensive side of the ball, a fumble is a very crucial mistake and can very well get that player benched for the remainder of the game. I was put to the test to finish the game because the

I've come to learn that fumbles in life will happen; the question is, will you be responsible for creating them or redeeming them? Even though it was human nature to get caught up in the moment, thinking of personal glory, I thought of someone else.

other guy had fumbled the ball. I've come to learn that fumbles in life will happen; the question is, will you be responsible for creating them or redeeming them? At first it seemed like the chance of a lifetime. I was able to go out and showcase my talent for all of the Pro-Scouts. I scored a touchdown so that my name would be etched into the record books forever on that date. But after I had my fun doing what I did best, something began to tug on my heart. The care, love, and compassion in my heart began to beat to a new tune in the middle of the game. Even though it was human nature to get caught up in the moment, thinking of personal glory, I thought of someone else.

During a timeout I jogged to the sidelines thinking about the other running back who had made a mistake and lost his chance to show the scouts what he was made of. So, I notified the coach that I was "tight" in my legs and told the coach I couldn't go anymore. I looked at the other running back and winked, and graciously, the other running back accepted this opportunity to get back onto the field.

It worked out for the good because he got back in the game and did rather well for himself, and all I could do was sit on the sideline with a huge smile. I was complete. The game I loved so much wasn't about pain at that moment, but it had brought me joy. I enjoyed the opportunity to play and compete, but I also was happy to let someone else try to change their own destiny too. This was a feeling that I cherish even now and has become a part of my principles. My heart beats better when I am making someone else's life better. I was able to leave behind an impressive record, thanks to God: I finished second on the Wildcats with 541 yards, six touchdowns, and 97 carries while playing in only 4-1/2 games (because I was out injured for the rest of the games). I currently hold three Kansas State Powercat strength records: 4.22 in the 40-yard dash, 42" in the vertical jump, and 42.04 in the 300-yard shuffle.

After that game was over, I had to go back to the real world, back to the grind. It was time to get ready for the NFL. As I was preparing and being tested by the NFL, another trial came into play. There were some who questioned whether I had what it took to be an NFL player. They didn't question my talent but my lifestyle. I was a Blue Chip player with a dark past. My troublesome teen years had resurfaced and were coming back to haunt me.

4

ANOTHER TEST

After the long wait, after all
the ups and the downs,
all the injuries and setbacks,
the time had finally come.

I went home with my head hung low that summer. The coaches and scouts had written me off. They told me that I wouldn't get picked up because I was too much of a risk for a team to take. They told me I had been in too much trouble and was too much of a thug. They thought I resembled a gang member. I had to dig deep to get over this stunning blow to my self-esteem.

My mother reminded me that only God could determine my future and that it wasn't in the hands of man because man is in the hands of God. Friends, parents, students, know that when man has written you out, God has permanently etched you in. He knows where He needs you, what position He needs you to play in this world, and what plays He wants you to run. No one can take God's playbook out of His hands. Your purpose is in safekeeping with Him!

I kept my mother's words in my heart and mind, only to realize that more pain was on the way. I was staying in shape and living my life the best I could. I was trying to forget about my past, trying to let go of the pain, the hurt, the agony, the defeat, and the lies that the naysayers had spoken about me.

The draft was fast approaching, and before I knew it, the night before the drafts had come. I was home getting ready for bed for my big day ahead. Right after I decided to call it a night, my phone rang.

"Frank, what's up, boy? This is Royce—come holla' at me at the club."

Being the good friend, I mustered up a little strength and decided to go and see my friend, who was hyped up that I was back in town. When I got outside to crank up my brand-new SUV, it wouldn't start. This would have been the perfect excuse to stay home for most friends, especially since it was about two in the morning. Instead, ever faithful, I got my dad out of bed and had him give me a jump start.

Finally, I arrived and we were able to catch up and make plans for later that day, which was Draft Day, the biggest day of my life to that point. After the quick reunion, I headed back home to try and get a little sleep before the draft started later that day. I woke up the next morning, expecting Royce and his brother to come over and watch the draft with me. Royce's brother showed up first, which was expected because of the late night Royce had. Royce's brother told me that Royce had told him he would just meet up with us, so we were both expecting him. A little while later, his brother got a call.

"Hey, man, I think this is your brother they are talking about on the news."

According to the news account, a young man in a Chevy had lost control of the wheel, gone off the road, and wrapped his car around a tree. We jumped in the car and went to see if it was Royce's car. Sure enough, when we arrived we saw that it was him. *Why me?* was all that flooded my mind. It was all I could ask the Lord. *Why me, Lord? I just saw him! I was just with him last night!* Rest in peace, Royce Jackson. Here was another tragedy on the day when I should have been excited and anticipating change. This was not the change I was expecting. I was devastated by this loss. I expected Royce to be there when I made it to the NFL. The pain of losing him was unbearable. He would call me every morning before my games at Kansas State and get me hyped up. He would call me early and even wake me up out of my sleep, jump-starting my game. I was battered but not broken; I felt beaten but not defeated. I held on for dear life.

I hoped for a better day, a day when my trials and tribulations would be over. But does that day ever really come? When you're headed for the end zone, your grip on the ball must be tight. There are some opponents whose sole job is to get you to loosen your grip and rip the victory from your hands. So it is in life. I've come to learn that as long as you are living, there will be trials, but when you feel like letting go, that is the time when you must grip hope, purpose, and life that much tighter.

My family and I gathered to watch the draft, but there was a dark cloud in the room all the while. Round

I've come to learn that as long as you are living, there will be trials. But when you feel like letting go, that is the time when you must grip hope, purpose, and life that much tighter.

after round and pick after pick, my name wasn't called. Then I got a phone call from the Kansas City Chiefs. They knew exactly who Frank Murphy Jr. was because they had watched me play for the last three seasons while I was in Kansas. They told me they were interested in me and might take me on their next pick. For some reason, they changed their minds at the last minute and didn't pick me. This was just another test, just a test to see if my hopes could be broken, to see if I had fixed my hope on an object or on God.

Instead of giving up all hope on the game I loved, I just endured the pain. Feeling a little down, I decided to turn the TV off and go take a nap. Then it came: in the sixth round the Chicago Bears selected Frank Murphy Jr., running back from Kansas State University.

Screams and tears of joy began to flow in the Murphy household. After the long wait, after all of the ups and downs, all the injuries and setbacks, the time had finally come. Frank Murphy Jr. was officially a part of the NFL.

That night, I went out and celebrated! I had new wheels, an Escalade, and I had left the party. That night, I was followed home from the hood to the suburbs. After I got out of the car and walked up to my friend's house, I saw one guy with a gun, and I tried to run. I was stopped by two men at the same time, with guns at both of my temples, and robbed at gunpoint. It was a setup. As they ordered me to get down, I didn't know if it was a random act or a vendetta. All I could think was, *Is it gonna end like this?* In Bang 'Em, Duval County, if you get robbed, you get shot. I felt immobilized, like in a trance. All I could hear was "Get down, Frank!" Finally, I got down on the ground, and they sped off. I immediately called my boys and we met up. That night, there was nothing on my boys' minds but to kill the guys who had robbed me.

The thieves took my truck, but they weren't the brightest of guys, having robbed me in a pretty decent part of town. The police nabbed them and I got my truck back, but my money was gone. I was furious. I planned to point them out and let my boys handle it, but when it came down to it, I began to struggle. My friends were desperate to take these guys out, but hustling wasn't my lifestyle anymore. In the end, I had to make a decision. I couldn't take the hood life with me.

In this new life I was about to enter, I didn't have to do this. I wasn't 100 percent certain of the guys who did it, and I didn't want my friends to take the wrong guys out and have innocent blood on my hands. I'm so thankful I made the right decision. This is where many would feel that the hardest part was over, but in actuality the hardest part was yet to come.

5

FANTASY TO REALITY

"I believe in him; I do very much so."

—Tony Dungy

Out of Control

We've often seen people involved in excess spending, no-holds-barred luxury, and no limits on what they spend or how they can do it. As I got ready to enter into the NFL, all I had heard was that it was all about the money, the fame, the women, and the parties. So, naturally, when I made it, I wanted my life to match up to these expectations.

There was something about the revelry that filled a void in my life. Something about it made me feel as if I had arrived or accomplished what it was I was expected to accomplish.

As soon as I arrived in Chicago, I organized a huge party. In a city that wasn't my home, in a city where I was all alone, I was the life of the party and the reason for the party.

In Jacksonville, it was no different. Boat parties, block parties, barbecues, club parties; where there was a party, you could expect me to be the host. It was all on me— all expenses paid. There was something about the revelry that filled a void in my life. Something about it made me feel as if I had arrived or accomplished what it was I was expected to accomplish. I partied until the sun came up. The sad part was that I had to go to camp and perform in the morning, but by then I was partied out.

I would be up all night until around five in the morning and then have to go out and practice all day. I was out of wind and exhausted at almost every practice. The coaches didn't know what my off-the-field life was like; all they knew was that it was showing on the field. I had the opportunity to compete for a starting spot or at least earn a lot of playing time, but I didn't prepare. It has been said that success happens when opportunity meets preparation. I wasn't successful with the Chicago Bears because I wasn't prepared. I've come to understand that 90 percent of your success is determined by your preparation.

The lifestyle that I was indulging in was all a fantasy. I was living a dream, not realizing that it could soon become a night-

> The lifestyle that I was indulging in was all a fantasy. I saw my present situation as my final destination instead of just a pit stop. So instead of building up to finish the race ahead, I was breaking down.

mare. I had quickly forgotten about how hard I had worked in Kansas to get to the professional arena. I saw my present situation as my final destination instead of just a pit stop. So instead of building up to finish the race ahead, I was breaking down.

I hadn't been told that I had to focus and not settle. I hadn't been told that this was just the beginning; instead, like so many new to the pros, I was told that I had arrived. Most people from my hometown would have been satisfied to just graduate from high school and a select few to graduate from college, but to make it to the NFL was only a dream. Some even joked that NFL stood for "Not For Long." I had "arrived," in my mind, and I was living a dream. I was a millionaire on paper in my twenties, but I lost it all. I had to climb back to the top by changing my character and walking by faith in God and not in my talent. My character would keep me where my talent was taking me.

Everything that I had heard about the NFL was right in front of me, attainable, without any holds barred, and I decided to indulge. It was almost like taking fruit from a forbidden tree because this new world changed my lifestyle so drastically. I lived like a celebrity, thought like a megastar, and was seen as an idol in my hometown. While my fame was rising, I was not taking into account the work ethic and time management it took to maintain that success.

I found out pretty fast that success wouldn't sustain itself. I had to get my priorities in order—and fast. The day finally came, the final cut for the Chicago Bears. I got on the phone and called my agent a day or two before. It was time to face a harsh reality.

"Hey, man, I think you ought to fly up here because they may let me go."

My agent arrived to accompany me on the day of the final cut. We were sitting in the hotel room waiting for the call. We knew that if I didn't get a call by a certain time, I had made the team. Anxiously, I was counting down the time. Right before the deadline, the phone rang. The coach had decided to keep me, but he wanted to put me on the practice team.

This would have been feasible, but I also got a call from the Tampa Bay Buccaneers. Coach Tony Dungy and Marc Dominik, the general manager, called, wanting me to come and play for them. All I could think about was that I would be playing with people I admired: Warren Sapp, Warrick Dunn, Mike Alstott, John Lynch, Derrick Brooks, Ronde Barber, Keyshawn Johnson, and Simeon Rice, some of the best players around. I met with the Bears' General Manager, and he offered me more than what a player on the practice squad gets, but it didn't sound as good as an opportunity to play for the Bucs. So I decided to go to the Bucs.

When I went to the Tampa Bay Buccaneers, I continued living my idea of the American dream. Sticking to the Not-For-Long lifestyle, I rushed headlong into the privileges of my status as a pro player. Since this dream was supposed to be short-lived, why not? This was my mentality, and many others in the NFL shared the same mind-set. When I arrived in Tampa, I had a meeting with Coach Tony Dungy. He told me that he was glad to have me, but if I got into any trouble he would have to let me go. He talked with me about my past and asked me what I had learned from it. I told him that I had learned two things: 1) it was important to have principles, and 2) where you hang and who you are with are equally important. I let him know that all I needed was a chance to show that I was a good person. I was so encouraged as Coach Dungy spoke about me to others.

"I believe in him, I do very much so," he told a *St.*

> I told him that I had learned two things: 1) it was important to have principles, and 2) where you hang and who you are with are equally important. I let him know that all I needed was a chance to show that I was a good person.

Petersburg Times reporter. I had and still have the utmost respect for Coach Dungy, and I didn't want to let him down. It was and is important for me even now to live up to those words and the expectation that was placed before me.

A New Ballgame

Although I lived hard off the field, this time I tried my best to work hard on the field as well. I would go out to a party, staying out all night; then, instead of going home, I would go to the sporting facility and sleep until it was time for practice so that I wouldn't be late. Of course, to someone passing by it would look like I had such dedication and love for the game that I even slept in the facility. In reality I was straddling the line between my responsibilities and the pleasures of life. I was living it up with cars, clothes, jewelry, and parties. Those trappings of newfound wealth meant more than football at this time in my life—and my lack of dedication showed up on the field. This was a very crucial time for me because Coach Dungy and his staff asked me to move from running back to wide receiver. All of my life I had carried the ball out of the back field, but now I was being asked to line up in the fast lane, to strap up with the speedsters and catch speeding bullets in the middle of traffic.

Wide receivers play an entirely different ballgame than running backs; it was a whole different beast. I had to learn the routes and how to catch the ball in traffic. I was super-fast, but I had to learn how to tame my speed and time my stride, like a choreographed dance between player and soaring pigskin. This was no easy task, to say the least.

To master a transition like this, a player would need to be completely focused on the task at hand. That player would have to eat, sleep, and drink their playbook. He would have to arrive early and leave late. He would have to watch hours of film and spend even more time than that actually practicing the craft. NFL wide receivers are pros for a reason: the majority of them have been doing it all their lives. So to ask a man to perform on the level of guys who had been doing it all their lives was an honor, a daunting prospect, and a challenging task. I had the ability to make this transition, and the Bucs staff knew that instantly and instinctively.

The missing link lay in my lifestyle off the field; this was where I was not up to par. My colleagues and I would leave right after practice to catch a plane to another city for a party and fly back in the next morning to make it to practice the next day. This wasn't unusual for some NFL players; this was the norm, and this was the life. The coaches didn't know this was going on, especially considering the millions that their organization was investing along with the fact that their professional reputations were on the line for poor performance as a result of undisciplined players. The NFL was more than just football; it was a lifestyle.

The National Football League was shaping me into a new man. I have found that money just amplifies who a person really is, and to a certain extent, I was arrogant before I went into the NFL. But when I got the money, it made me ten times worse. I would talk down to people around me; money was changing my attitude and how I interacted with people. It was going to my head and taking control of my life; money became my biggest vice. I would spend $5,000 here, $10,000 there on diamonds and clothes. I had become a shopaholic; it made me feel good, and I loved it.

> I have found that money just amplifies who a person really is, and to a certain extent, I was arrogant before I went into the NFL. But when I got the money, it made me ten times worse.

On the field, that first season with the Bucs was a growing process. The Bucs saw potential in me, and they decided to let my talent blossom. I was trying to make a name for myself in the NFL and in the Bucs organization. I was an intense guy on the field, so obviously fights would occur. But I also used my intensity and charisma to build lifelong relationships; one of those relationships was with Coach Dungy, which extends to this day. I would get to know the powers that be, and by cultivating good relationships I felt that those relationships kept me around longer than some people feel I should have been.

I played hard whenever I got the chance, and I did enough to get by. That season the Bucs made it to the playoffs only to lose to the Philadelphia Eagles. Things would begin to change after that loss, however. That night while we were on the plane ride home, I had a gut feeling that someone was going to lose their job. It just so happened to be the offensive coordinator. Gratefully, it stopped there and my job was spared. I lived to see another season with the Bucs.

The next season came, and I was playing under Coach Dungy again. I felt that I was trying to learn and trying to grow, not only as a new wide receiver, but as a man also. It wouldn't be that easy. I made it through training camp with character and a hard fight. I found it hard to explain why I was so arrogant toward the other guys who weren't going to make the team, but it shows how much I still had to grow.

In a sense, I was operating under a grace that I didn't really comprehend but that I could feel. To hide my insecurities, I would tease the other guys who weren't as fast or as big or as fortunate as I was. We would be eating and here I would come, exercising my funny streak at their expense. All you could hear were laughs and some guys telling me to chill out.

> I felt that I was trying to learn and trying to grow, not only as a new wide receiver, but as a man also. It wouldn't be that easy.

Truthfully and painfully, all along I was hiding the fear I had of being cut. It is a feeling that is common in pro football, a feeling that you are just hanging on by a thread of luck, and at any moment you could be injured or do the wrong thing and get cut from the team. So sometimes in order to hide your fear, you just had to find something to laugh about. I realize that I wasn't a downright mean guy; I just liked to laugh and see others smile, but sometimes I diverted my fears and worries at the expense of others. Anyone who really knows me knew that if any one of the guys whom I teased needed anything, I would have been there for them. I was a work in progress.

However, no matter how good we are, when we mix it with bad, there is always a price we pay. It wasn't until later that I would realize I would reap everything I sowed, and the same things I jokingly said about others, people would say about me. It was nothing more and nothing less. Usually the way pro football works is that there is always a spot in the NFL for a guy who is six foot, 215 pounds, running a 4.2 in the 40 and benching 450 pounds. I was big, strong, and fast—what coach wouldn't want an athlete of that caliber? It became evident that what I was going through on and off the field was designed by God to be a building process for me, preparing me for what was to come.

That second season under Coach Dungy, the Bucs repeated their history and went to the play-offs and lost to the Philadelphia Eagles yet again. That same look was in the eyes of the staff on the ride home, and dread hovered thick among us. I had the same thoughts from the year before. *Someone is going to lose their job,* I thought to

It became evident that what I was going through on and off the field was a building process. Something bigger than me was preparing me for what was to come.

myself. It wasn't long after that game that Coach Dungy was released. Wow! This was a blow to the whole team, especially me.

Coach Dungy had given me a chance that no other coach would have given me. He kept me for two whole seasons, something no other coach would do for a guy like me. I am grateful to Coach Dungy for the chance. I felt they should have given him more time to grow and learn as their head coach. He was and still is a man in whom I never found a fault. He never demonstrated a weakness or a flaw in his character in all his dealings with us. He was and continues to be an awe-inspiring man, and others would recognize that after he went on to coach the NFL Indianapolis Colts and lead them to the Super Bowl victory.

The overriding question in my life at that time was, what would I do now that my saving grace was gone? The new coach was a young fireball by the name of Coach John Gruden, the total opposite of my former one. He would get up in your face and yell at the top of his lungs with his face turning bright red.

"What are you doing? You don't have a clue, do you?"

Gruden was a blunt, straight talker, determined to pull the best out of you. Coach Gruden pushed me and made me a better player. He made me dig deeper than I had ever dug both physically and mentally in order to get prepared for a game. Gruden was always fired up so that kept me fired up, and it brought out a passion and zeal in me that I had never experienced before. Without that bond that I had with Coach Dungy, this would have become all about business. Coach Gruden wasn't going to look inside of the man; all he was concerned with was what you could do on the field. I figured I would show him.

It was game time for our first preseason game, and the Bucs were set to receive the kick. Coach Gruden was getting ready to see the first play as the Bucs' head coach. I was on the field back deep for the Bucs with my 4.2 speed rumbling like a Porsche engine revving up.

The ball was kicked high and deep. I bounced around while the ball was in the air, gauging the distance, the seconds feeling like eternity, then boom! The ball shot me square in my chest, and I tucked it in and took off. My stride was long and my steps were fast! I saw a seam and the field parted like the Red Sea. I hit it fast and hard. I was gone to glory! I sailed into the end zone practically untouched for a 96-yard return. What a welcome for Coach Gruden! I returned that kick on the first play of the game to make a statement about my ability and set the tone for my interaction. That return asked, *Am I the type of guy you need on your team?* Would that be enough?

The answer was a resounding no! That wasn't enough for Coach Gruden and his staff apparently because they released me by the end of the preseason. I got injured in the third preseason game, and they sent me on my way.

I stayed in Tampa and continued to train and rehab. It took about six weeks to get back up to my usual level of play. During my training, many felt that I should call it quits or give up, but I was determined to press on and move forward through my pain and my disappointments. Nothing was gonna get me down.

I was in the middle of an upper body set when I received an unexpected call from the Houston Texans and signed with them. There were five games left in their season when they brought me on. I finished the year up with them, breaking a record by having five tackles on Special Teams in one game. But at the end of the season, the coach called me into the office.

"Frank, we thank you for your services; if we need you again, we will bring you back."

I thanked him, and just like that I was let go—this was how the business worked. Off the field, I hadn't grown much. I was still partying and having fun, spending money, shopping for clothes, entertaining women, living the life. I was still a work in progress, and it was almost as if God were sending me messages, trying to see what it would take to make me get my life right off the field but getting cut from a team didn't seem to be enough.

Back Home Again

By 2003, I was back home in Jacksonville, watching and waiting. I was trying to get back into the NFL and trying to call every team myself and put my name in the ears of the coaches. That didn't work, but I didn't lose the faith. I believed that there was something more for me and that something would happen. So I gave my agent a call.

"Hey, man; I had a vision that I'm gonna be back with the Bucs."

It was a few months later when I got a call from the Bucs.

"Hey, guy—we wantcha. You don't even have to work out. We know what you can do."

I got on the road and headed to Tampa right away. During this season I was on the field and playing like normal, and off the field, I was still out of control. I was hosting parties and being the life of the party scene. I was still addicted to that lifestyle.

One would think that after my layoff I would have made some drastic changes, but instead, I was still falling for the temptation and taking the bait. Through it all, God was still trying to reach me, a young man who knew of Him but was lost amidst the pull of an unrestrained lifestyle.

After the first four games, I was leading in kick return yards, and then we played a game against the Denver Broncos. On this day, no one but God knew that I would get injured again. I popped my Achilles' tendon, and I was told there was a great chance I wouldn't return to the field. This injury took a huge toll on me. It had me out for an entire year. But I was determined to make it back to the field, so I worked and rehabilitated as hard as I could.

> Through it all, God was still trying to reach me, a young man who knew of Him but was lost amidst the pull of an unrestrained lifestyle.

In that year I would go through a change. I felt like it was time for it. I was getting ready to move back to Jacksonville, but my friend said I could move in with

him, and so it was back to the hood. I moved there to
lie low. This was a place where I could hide out, and
people wouldn't know what I was doing or where I was.
They wouldn't be able to laugh at me or talk down to
me. I wouldn't be hounded or asked questions I didn't
yet have the answers to. It was in my shame that I
would find strength, and my life would finally change.

6

THE BIGGER PICTURE

I realized, looking back, that obeying
God was more important
than my natural desire.

Spiritual Rehab

Spiritual Rehab is the phrase I would coin to describe this time of change in my life. I had been up and down over and over again, but this was the lowest I had ever felt. In the beginning of this season of change, I felt that it was the end of the road and that it was all over, but God said something different.

I began to see the bigger picture. It was bigger than just football; it was bigger than me; this was spiritual warfare. There was a battle going on for my very life. There was a battle going on for my mind, body, and soul.

> I began to see the bigger picture. It was bigger than just football; it was bigger than me; this was spiritual warfare. There was a battle going on for my very life. There was a battle going on for my mind, body, and soul.

As much as I was suffering natural injury and rehab, I was suffering spiritual injury as well, only up to this point, I hadn't been providing much rehab to my spirit man—I was caught between good and evil. It was the tug of the temptations of the world against the tug of my Christian upbringing. I already knew God in the general sense; my mother was a praying mother and she oftentimes spoke the Word into my life. I had walked with God in Kansas, and God had delivered me many times before. Looking back over my life, all I could say was that it was by God's grace that I had made it through as well as I did. From the bullets that flew past my face, the robbery in Jacksonville, the parties, the fights, the trials that I won—only God could have brought me through safely.

During this "Spiritual Rehab," I was in a place of desolation. I was back in the hood around the drugs and the violence. There were nights when I felt a very strong urge to be with different women, to go out and drink at parties. But instead, I stayed in and prayed my way through; I was like an addict suffering from withdrawals of my former lifestyle. In a cold sweat, I would cry out to the Lord. For more than six months I was being cleansed and deprogrammed, even to the point of getting rid of my digital black book. I was able to let God break the strongholds the devil had on my life. God took away the youthful lust; He took away the desire for the night life and the alcohol.

God humbled me and taught me the essence of brotherhood. I learned that I couldn't do this by myself; I leaned on the strength of my roommates, who encouraged me to deny myself and resist temptation. We learned to strengthen each other, and it made us better. During this period, I became a new creature. My spiritual slate was wiped clean in a way I had not experienced before.

> **I can boldly say with confidence and experience that no matter how much money you have, how many friends you have, how much worldly success you have, nothing matters unless you have God as your foundation.**

I felt like the prodigal son returning home. I had decided at my entrance into the NFL that I would forsake God and go my own way. I had always depended on the money and the lifestyle to get me by. I mean, after all, who needs God when you have money? That's what many people think and are even led to believe, and that's where they go wrong. They develop a sense of false security. I can boldly say with confidence and experience that no matter how much money you have, how many friends you have, how much worldly success you have, nothing matters unless you have God as your foundation.

I've learned that the only real thing in life is developing a real relationship with Jesus Christ; His life is more real than the material world if we would simply hand over our self-determined course. I was attending church but not consistently. It was during this time that I began to grow and develop a closer relationship with God under the leadership of Pastor Greg Powe, founder of Revealing Truth Ministries.

I confessed my faults, gave up my old ways, and decided to put my life in the hands of God. It was at my lowest point that God blessed me the most. Everyone around thought I would be losing my mind or going crazy, but God gave me peace that surpassed all understanding. I was a walking testament to change.

Those around me could see God in me working through me. One friend constantly encouraged me to get rooted and grounded in love to see great results. It became a mantra to me, and to this day we are still friends. God changed me and gave me another chance at life, not just life here on earth, but eternal life.

As my "Spiritual Rehab" continued, I was able to enter the real estate business. As I look back, I realize that God showed up without fail. In 2005, while I was out of the NFL, I did well financially. My life began to change for the better. God had welcomed me back like the prodigal son. He sent the finest of things as He restored me. He showed up in my life in unmistakable ways.

This house in the hood was my personal wilderness, a place where I could escape, much like the places where men of God would escape to in the Bible. Sometimes we have to get away and separate ourselves from everyone else in order for God to reach us and for us to hear God speak. In my wilderness, God showed up and spoke to me and gave me new life.

At that time, I got a call from the Miami Dolphins for the 2006 season. I got there late in camp, after everyone else had already been there. I felt a little apprehensive about going. This was my number-one party spot, the place where I would kick it with my boys. Everyone was expecting the old Frank. I expressed that I was living for God, but they didn't believe me. It was different this time, though. Instead of going to the club and throwing a huge party upon my arrival like I would do in the past, I went right to work, on and off the field. On the field I was playing my heart out. Off the field, I was witnessing about the goodness of God, how God had changed my life, and how He could change the lives of my teammates.

I remember I was in the locker room playing one of my favorite gospel artists, Canton Jones, and my team started jammin' to it. I came in as a leader, encouraging and praying for others. I was rooming with another guy, and I wasn't feeling it. I was going to do what it took to get a private room, but God had it set up that there were no other rooms. My roommate couldn't believe all the things I had given up. Finally, after listening to my testimony, he broke down and revealed that he had been struggling with a drug addiction. I felt humbled in that moment. Here I was, trying to get my own room, and God had other plans. I went to the restroom and prayed for him. When I came out, he lay there crying.

As I look back, I thought I was going to play, but God had sent me there for other reasons. It wasn't time for me to simply enjoy personal time with the Lord, but it was ministry time, time to let God use me. When I saw my roommate later on, we hugged and both thanked God.

> I had faced my fears and temptations, and recognized that the things that used to move me and persuade me no longer held any power over me. There was a peace—through the wilderness, I had grown.

I had faced my fears and temptations, and recognized that the things that used to move me and persuade me no longer held any power over me. There was a peace—through the wilderness, I had grown. God had something different for me, though.

After the second preseason game, Coach Nick Saban called me in and told me that they were going to release me. The coach said he really didn't know why he was releasing me except for the fact that they had to make a cut, and I was the last guy to come in. It wouldn't be fair to the other guys who had been there throughout the entire camp to get cut before I did. I felt a peace about the matter. I was thankful for the opportunity to go to camp, and I told the coach so. Then I went on about my business.

As I was leaving, I was going back to Tampa, but the Spirit led me to go to Jacksonville instead. After conferring with my pastor, I headed on. As soon as I hit Jacksonville, I felt peace, but I received a call. My father was dying. I sped to the hospital. I left my Benz and ran to the room. When I got there, I asked everyone to leave except my mother. I believe God wanted everyone who doubted to get out of the room. I asked my father if he wanted to live. He said yes, and then my mother and I prayed for about twenty-five minutes. I walked out and went home, much to my family's surprise and protests. I told them my father was healed.

After I left, I snapped out of it, thinking, *What just*

happened? It had to have been the Spirit of God that moved me. No one had touched my car, and all was well. I realized, looking back, that obeying God was more important than my natural desires. God had taken me out of myself and my personal needs so that He could use me. It wasn't yet time for my father to leave this earth.

I moved back to Jacksonville to continue training and getting ready for another pickup. I was walking with the Lord and loving life. I started a real estate business in Jacksonville and continued to establish my relationship with God. He was with me, sustaining me through it all.

7

FINDING
PURPOSE

"Frank, you gonna pray?"

The CFL

I was outside my parents' home in Callahan when I received a call from the pro personnel of the Toronto Argonauts. As a result I signed a deal with them and started training immediately, getting ready for the season. Much different from the NFL, they were part of the CFL (Canadian Football League). There are various other international leagues that a player can sign with. I was signed to the team to play a year with them. Ultimately I wanted to get more game tape for the NFL. I needed to be able to showcase myself, and the CFL would allow me the platform to do just that.

Toronto, Canada, was breathtakingly beautiful. I came late in the preseason, but I hit the ground full-speed. I led the team in many areas at the receiver position. I racked up stats and made some good film for the NFL to see. I came; I saw; I conquered. I worked within the community, made friends there, and enjoyed my time with the Canadians. Soon, it was time for me to head back to Florida and the roller-coaster ride of the NFL.

Finding Purpose

I arrived home and began training right away at a facility in Tampa. Michael Vick's agent was there watching his quarterback while I was playing receiver for the quarterback. After we were done, I asked how Vick was doing and his agent expressed that he was doing well, but he wanted Vick to connect with Coach Dungy. He was getting the run-around with contact information. Immediately, I thought of how I could be of service. I dialed up Coach Dungy and asked for permission to give his information to the agent, who would then connect him with Michael Vick. Coach Dungy was excited. A few days later, it hit the news that Coach Dungy was meeting with Michael Vick and mentoring him. I had a feeling that God was in the middle of it, and I was thankful for the opportunity to be at the right place and time to be used by Him.

I was anticipating a call from the Texans, and when it finally came, they told me to be ready, that they would call me back in two weeks to come up for the season. I reorganized my life, kicked it into high gear, and got prepared for the call, but the call never came.

After Houston didn't call, I decided to return to the Argonauts. They signed me back, and I prepared and trained. The trip back to the CFL was long and extensive. Four hours after I finally had arrived in Canada, reunited with players, and gotten settled into my hotel room, I received a call from personnel saying they no longer needed my services. When I got off the phone after encouraging them, I prayed.

I should have been mad and disappointed, but I took the focus off of me. I wondered, *God, who is it that I'm here for? Who is it I'm supposed to witness to?* I began to walk around the hotel, talking to other players and staying alert to God's move.

Soon my limo driver arrived, and I settled in to return to the airport. I struck up a conversation with the driver, who wondered why I was leaving. As I began to share with him, my limo driver responded:

"Frank, you came here for me. I've been contemplating suicide."

I began to witness to him, and we pulled over to the side of the road. I began to minister to him, letting him know that God cared about him. As I left to get on the plane, the driver let me know that I had saved his life. I explained to him that it was all God, and if for no other reason, God had sent me there for him and that God loved him. I let him know that he was on to something great! As I got on the plane, I remembered God's promises to me that I would be playing this year. I knew there was more to the situation than this!

The UFL

I went to Chattanooga, Tennessee, and began a career at the Peyton Manning Training Facility. While I began to personally train others, I began to get myself in top form too. As I trained there, I got a call from Jay Gruden, brother to John Gruden of the Tampa Bay Bucs, and head coach of the Florida Tuskers. He called me at the D1 Facility unexpectedly.

"Frank, have you heard about the new league? Man, I want you to come play."

I signed with the UFL to play for the Florida Tuskers. It was less games, yet they were offering more money. This was a chance to let my light shine. Ironically, I had not yet told anyone there that I had changed my life and was now living for Jesus (what is commonly known as being saved). As I walked around being myself, I will never forget our first game. It was time to pray before the game, and so we all bowed our heads. Nobody said anything. I just happened to look up and everybody was looking at me. Then it came:

> I bowed my head and led them in prayer. It was then that I knew that it was the way you lived your life that made a difference. I guess people were watching me.

"Frank, you gonna pray?"

I bowed my head and led them in prayer. It was then that I knew that it was the way you lived your life that made a difference. I guess people were watching me. I didn't go out and party. I don't know what all played into their decision, but from that day on, I began to wake up at 5:30 a.m. and go pray for my team for the season. During this time, I was in the top five in special team tackles and second in touchdowns. Since they were a brand new team, I scored the first touchdown in the Florida Tuskers' history. They asked me to autograph the ball and send it to the owner after the game. I also scored the last touchdown in the championship game. After this, I returned to Chattanooga, Tennessee.

"Lord, I'll follow."

Upon my return, I began to work once more with the D1 Training Facility in Chattanooga, which was owned by Peyton Manning, who one day would become the future Hall of Famer for the Indianapolis Colts. I trained professional athletes and high school athletes, as well as women, assisting them in weight loss. I used this time to mentor athletes and teach them concerning the things that were ahead and the potential traps that could be set in their path. I trained groups of women, three hours at a time. At the same time, I ministered to both the women and men.

Then I was offered a position as a high school coach at Baylor School, one of the most prestigious schools in America with world-class facilities, on a par with collegiate standards. I stepped in as a receiver coach, helped with the team workout program, and mentored the team once a week. I began to empower them with skills they would need for both making it in the pros and living a purposeful life. After about two weeks, I received a call from the UFL. The Omaha Nighthawks called.

"Can you fly out tomorrow?"

I was elated, happily agreeing. I hung up the phone, thinking, *Man, this is awesome!* I sat down to reflect, and it hit me. All I could see were the kids' faces flashing across my mind. *Man, I can't go. I can't leave these kids like this. I have to finish what I've started.* I realized I could have hurt the youth whom God had sent me to mentor and care for with my haste to rush off to play.

It's Time for Ministry

I called the general manager back, thanked him for the opportunity, but told him I'd decided against returning to play. I had never turned down a football contract before, but that day I knew it was time for ministry. This was when my ministry started. I would mentor the team both through one-on-one sessions and the Soaring With Eagles Program that I founded. My focus was no longer on me but on God and how I could make a difference in the lives of those around me. I had people declaring me a fool, thinking I was stupid not to go back and play because this was an opportunity to get back in the NFL.

But I cared about the kids. I had never felt this way before, and it changed my life. After the season ended, my purpose expanded, and I began preparing for the next move with God.

This is what I have been created to do! I've been placed in a position to help young boys and men who find themselves in some of the very same situations I had found myself. I can give them an answer and a way out!

I will be serving and teaching men in an even greater capacity under the leadership of Pastor Greg Powe. I will be helping youth and men through the Gathering of Champions program in Tampa, empowering them to change their lives. I will be intervening in the lives of juvenile offenders who have been certified as adults, too young to recognize the impact that time in jail will have on their futures. This is what I have been created to do! I've been placed in a position to help young boys and men who find themselves in some of the very same situations I had found myself. I can give them an answer and a way out! Isn't God great?

As I reflect on what God did in me, I am overwhelmed. He groomed me in Tennessee to be a greater witness and mentor to thousands. He took me through a process, and because I was obedient to God, there is so much in store for me!

When I was preparing for the NFL, things began to happen in my life off the field. This is where I began to see God working in a different way, and I began to realize that I was much more than just an NFL player. I began to have flashbacks of a vision I had years ago. This vision was one about having a men's conference where I would partner with other professional athletes in different cities, with Pastor Greg Powe, and with coaches like Tony Dungy and Jim Cartwell (now head coach of the Indianapolis Colts), to reach out to men of all ages and provide powerful seminars that would impact and change lives.

I can't contain all that God is doing, but know this: if He did it for me, He can do it for you! It took me saying, "Yes, Lord, I'll go. Yes, Lord, I'll follow." As soon as I said yes, boom, it began happening.

In the summer of 2010, I worked with D1 Training Facility and directed football camps for Pro Camps Worldwide. I was training and catching balls from two future Hall of Famers—Peyton Manning and Tom Brady (New England Patriots). I was the director at Adrian Peterson's camp, Reggie Bush's camp, Peyton Manning's camp, Steve Smith's camp, Devin Hester's camp, Chris Johnson's camp, Anthony Munyo's camp, Wes Welker's camp, and Matt Ryan's camp, just to name a few. The phenomenal thing was that I did more than teach: I ministered at these camps, speaking about my past and how I learned from my mistakes.

> As I ministered in these camps, I realized that the NFL was just a chapter in my life, one I am grateful for, but not the whole book. There was a purpose given to me from the day I was born, and now I am walking in that purpose.

These were great guys and young men. God gave me awesome ministry opportunities. I held power sessions on life skills. I'll never forget after one training session, a young guy came to me afterward and said, "I've been selling drugs. How do I stop?" From that point on, I recall more guys coming up afterward to ask me questions on different issues.

It's BIGGER Than This

As I ministered in these camps, I realized that the NFL was just a chapter in my life, one I am grateful for, but not the whole book. There was a purpose given to me from the day I was born, and now I am walking in that purpose. Football and the NFL provided a platform for me, provided and strengthened my character, and kept me out of trouble. It also provided an opportunity for me to meet the people whom God would have me to work with. My purpose is bigger than me; it's bigger than football; it's bigger than status—it's so much bigger!

As I look back over the events in my life, I realize that every single thing that happened to me was allowed

As I look back over the events in my life, I realize that every single thing that happened to me was allowed by God, and that all of it will play a part in my lifelong ministry.

by God, and that all of it will play a part in my lifelong ministry. Had I not been through it, I wouldn't have somewhere to get to. Had I not been knocked down, I wouldn't have been able to get up. Had I not experienced the pain and the suffering, the agony of defeat, the loneliness of being isolated, the despair of having a bad name, I would have no story of how my life was changed to share with some people desperately in need of it. But because I've been through it, I am able to teach and share some of the power playbook with others. I am telling this story across the nation so others won't have to go through what I went through.

To me, the NFL used to mean "Not For Long," but now it means "Necessary For Life." I needed the skills, the mentorship, the hard lessons, to make me the man I am today. My purpose is not one of my own, and it is humbling to know that God can take the sport that I am passionate about and wrap it up inside of His will so that I can do more than put on a great field performance, but also introduce others to the Ultimate Head Coach.

At this point there is no turning back; there is no giving up; the mission must be completed. The time is now because tomorrow won't wait! Will Frank play in the NFL? Big question mark. Will Frank play in any pro league? Big question mark. Will Frank continue to minister? Always.

8

POWER
PLAYS

The NFL saved my life

If you've ever had a compelling energy or desire to let off some steam, then you will agree with me that the sports arena is a great avenue by which to do that. As a youth, I was involved in various kinds of sports. These activities beyond academics literally saved my life. They gave me something to focus on that was positive. Here are some reasons why involving yourself in athletics is a great idea and could change your life, whether you are young or old. I want to shed some light on the positive things the NFL, CFL, UFL and other good sports programs can do:

Positive Results From a Good Sports Program

- It gave me something to look forward to each day.

- It gave me a second family.

- It built discipline and drew out discipline in me.

- It taught me how to live and eat healthier.

- It allowed me to understand vision.

- It helped me to understand my God-given purpose.

- It kept me active, pulling me away from the • thug lifestyle.

- It gave me another option over what my environment offered.

- It made me mentally tougher through adversity and trials.

- It taught me to use my anger as a tool, not a weapon.

- It gave me the opportunity to impact youth.

Counted Out and Disqualified

I write to you—my fellow athlete, student, parent, teacher, or coach—who have been counted out or disqualified. As you read my story, I'm sure you could see where I had counted myself out and done things that should have disqualified me and rightly so. I am so thankful that God didn't give up on me! You might be thinking, *Frank, you can't identify, but trust me, I feel you on this.* A lot of times, people feel that they can discount you because you haven't taken their road to success. Here are some things that fit the traditional success model:

- Having a degree

- Having a high grade point average

- Speaking eloquently

- Having a clean past, free from mistakes

- Having a good family history

- Achieving a great résumé of accomplishments and awards

- Maintaining a great credit history

There's nothing wrong with the traditional way, for these are important standards—but this is not the only way. Don't stop working toward your goals if you don't fit the traditional mold. Some may look at these markers of success and see that they have failed them all. By nature, we want people to take the path we carve out for them. (Parents, we especially can be guilty of wanting our children to be everything we weren't, in spite of the fact that God may have a different call on their lives.)

Know this, if you feel disqualified, remember that God is your Manufacturer. If you have been playing the role of disqualifier, you might be overlooking treasure because you are too focused on traditions. Learn to respect individual paths. We come from God; we come through a family to provide a service to this world. It's not who you come through, but it's who you come from.

Tips for Life at the Top

As a pro player for various teams, I've gained experience, knowledge, and physical stamina through learning from personal life lessons and sitting under the leadership of some of the NFL's greatest coaches. Here are some tips for staying at the top of your game even if you've come from the bottom of the draft.

How To Stay at the Top of Your Game

• Go where you are celebrated, not tolerated.

• You must define your name—neither your parents nor anyone else can do this for you.

• You can pray farther than you can see—faith in prayer goes further.

• Know the difference between fantasy and reality.

• Don't run from pressure but work through it.

• The eyes see only what the mind is ready to comprehend.

• Not knowing your purpose is like not knowing your name.

• The first part of changing is searching for something different.

- Never make a permanent decision based on a temporary situation.

- A true leader becomes a living billboard for others to see.

- The mirror is not just to reflect, but also to correct what you see.

- When you fail, fail forward not backward.

- Loving others is the key to your door of peace.

- Don't let your God-purpose go to the grave—live it and complete it.

- Growth will not take place without correction.

- A successful life is a series of good decisions made along the way.

- Living begins when you turn to what is higher than self—God.

- Learn to love yourself first before you try to love others.

- Life is bigger than you.

- Keep your eyes on what's before you, not what's with you—keep movin'.

- Cry when it hurts so bad and when it feels so good— it's good for the soul.

- You can't do 50 percent and expect 100 percent.

- Hard work pays off in the end.

- Obeying the rules leaves you with fewer regrets.

Steps to a Personal Power Play

I want to share with you eight steps I took to walk in the life I now walk in. It was like catching that ball, tucking it in, and heading for the end zone. Every day, I get the opportunity to make a touchdown, a lasting impact, because I am fulfilling my purpose.

1. Become a Christian. Life begins when you make Jesus Christ your personal Savior (see Romans 10:9–10).

2. Forgive others and yourself for the wrongs that have been committed against you.

3. Reprogram your mind regarding how you think and make decisions.

4. Put yourself around the right people.

5. Be a lifelong learner—gain more wisdom on how to live/do right.

6. Share your mistakes and victories with others to help them grow.

7. Don't quit and you won't be defeated!

8. Put action to the power plays above—simply do it!

FRANK & FRIENDS

Dwight Freeney, NFL All Pro Defensive End, Indianapolis Colts

Reggie Bush, NFL Tailback, Miami Dolphins

Steve Smith, NFL All Pro Wide Receiver, Carolina Panthers

Wes Welker, NFL All Pro Wide Receiver, New England Patriots

Adrian Peterson, NFL All Pro Running Back, Minnesota Vikings

EARLY YEARS

Frank at nine years old

Eleven years old, West Side Giants Little League, Jacksonville, Florida

Fifteen years old, West Nassau High Warriors, Running Back

Seventeen years old with his mom, Velma Murphy, All Star Game 1995

Frank with his dad, Frank Sr.

Frank receives his diploma from Garden City Community College

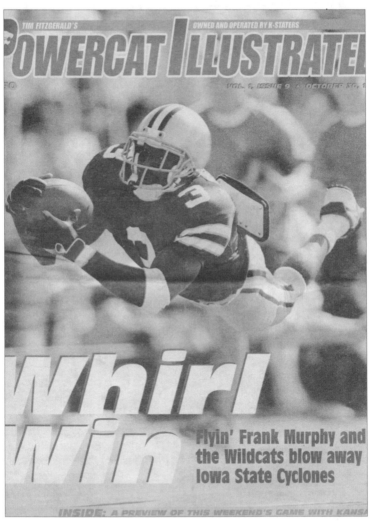

"Flyin' Frank Murphy" at Kansas State

Murphy fitting in fine with the Argos as number one Wide Receiver

Kansas State Running Back Frank D. Murphy outruns his opponent

Frank's workout DVDs

About the Author

Born in Jacksonville, Florida, to Velma and Franklin D. Murphy Sr., Frank D. Murphy overcame numerous ups and downs to live out his lifelong dream of playing professional football. Throughout high school, Murphy won numerous awards as the senior running back and return specialist at West Nassau High School: All-American, All State, and Player of the Year.

Murphy spent his first two years of college football playing for Itawamba Community College and Garden City Community College. He was subsequently named to the National Junior College Athletic Association All-American first team and National Player of the Year. Murphy then transferred to college football powerhouse, Kansas State University in 1998. Murphy currently holds three Powercat Strength Records: 4.22 in the 40 yard dash, 42" vertical jump, and 42.04 300 yard shuttle. Murphy was inducted into the National Junior College Hall of Fame in 2008.

After a successful collegiate football career, Murphy was drafted by the Chicago Bears in 2000. Murphy suited up for numerous teams throughout his professional NFL career as a running back, wide receiver, and return specialist for the Tampa Bay Buccaneers, Miami Dolphins, and the Houston Texans. Murphy also played in the Canadian Football League for the Toronto

Argonauts, and in the United Football League for Florida Tuskers.

Murphy has always been a supporter of programs that educate and empower people to realize their dreams and live their best lives. Throughout his career, Murphy has held numerous football camps, workshops, and toy drives for disadvantaged youth. Murphy has received numerous awards and recognitions for his community service initiatives, including the Key to the City of Callahan, Florida. He is the founder of Frank D. Murphy Charity, an organization dedicated to serving disadvantaged communities. As an ordained evangelist under Pastor Greg Powe of Revealing Truth Ministries, he lives to motivate and inspire people of all ages to realize their true potential and make a positive difference in the world for Jesus Christ.

For more information, or to contact the author:
visit: www.frankdmurphy.com
www.powerupbody.com or
www.frankdmurphycharity.org
phone: 1.800.618.4686
or email: frankdmurphybook@gmail.com